ARTISTS

A$AP ROCKY

MASTER **COLLABORATOR**

BY JUDY DODGE CUMMINGS

Essential Library

An Imprint of Abdo Publishing
abdobooks.com

ABDOBOOKS.COM

Published by Abdo Publishing, a division of ABDO, PO Box 398166, Minneapolis, Minnesota 55439. Copyright © 2020 by Abdo Consulting Group, Inc. International copyrights reserved in all countries. No part of this book may be reproduced in any form without written permission from the publisher. Essential Library™ is a trademark and logo of Abdo Publishing.

Printed in the United States of America, North Mankato, Minnesota.
092019
012020

Cover Photo: Evan Agostini/Invision/AP Images
Interior Photos: Sterling Munksgard/Shutterstock Images, 4–5, 94–95; Eddy Risch/
Keystone/AP Images, 6; Robb Cohen/Invision/AP Images, 10, 84; Shutterstock
Images, 13, 18–19, 88–89; Amy Harris/Invision/AP Images, 14; Frank Franklin II/AP
Images, 22; Andrew Chin/Getty Images Entertainment/Getty Images, 24–25; John
Ricard/BET/Getty Images Entertainment/Getty Images, 28–29; Andrew Morales/
Rex Features, 32; Steven Lawton/Getty Images Entertainment/Getty Images,
36–37; Chad Batka/Contour/Getty Images, 39; Charles Sykes/Invision/AP Images,
42; Roger Kisby/Getty Images Entertainment/Getty Images, 45; Tim Mosenfelder/
Getty Images Entertainment/Getty Images, 46; Matt Sayles/Invision/AP/Rex
Features, 49, 74; Kathy Hutchins/Shutterstock Images, 50, 65; RMV/Rex Features, 53,
93; Wade Payne/Invision/AP Images, 55; Michael Kovac/The Recording Academy/
Getty Images Entertainment/Getty Images, 56; Zachary Mazur/Getty Images
Entertainment/Getty Images, 59; iStockphoto, 62; RSAA/ZDS/Ricky Swift/WENN/
Newscom, 67; Thibault Camus/AP Images, 68, 73; Darren Gerrish/WireImage/Getty
Images, 71; Lionel Hahn/Sipa USA/AP Images, 78; David Wolff - Patrick/Redferns/
Getty Images, 87

Editor: Megan Ellis
Series Designer: Laura Graphenteen

LIBRARY OF CONGRESS CONTROL NUMBER: 2019942082
PUBLISHER'S CATALOGING-IN-PUBLICATION DATA

Names: Dodge Cummings, Judy, author.
Title: A$AP Rocky: master collaborator / by Judy Dodge Cummings
Other title: master collaborator
Description: Minneapolis, Minnesota : Abdo Publishing, 2020 | Series: Hip-hop
    artists | Includes online resources and index.
Identifiers: ISBN 9781532190179 (lib. bdg.) | ISBN 9781532176029 (ebook)
Subjects: LCSH: A$AP Rocky (Rapper), 1988- (Rakim Mayers)--Juvenile literature. |
    Rap (Music)--Juvenile literature. | Songwriters--Juvenile literature. | Actors--
    Juvenile literature. | Clothing models--Juvenile literature.
Classification: DDC 782.421649--dc23

CONTENTS

BREAKING OUT OF THE BOX

On May 20, 2018, a crowd gathered in a high-ceilinged room on the sixth floor of Sotheby's in New York, New York. Sotheby's is an auction house known for selling art, jewelry, and real estate to wealthy people. A gigantic cube sat in the middle of the room, its sides covered with white cloth so the inside of the box remained a mystery. Behind a counter on one side of the room sat a man and woman posing as scientists in white lab coats.

Some of the people wandering around the cube looked like typical Sotheby's customers dressed in luxury brand clothing. But others wore jeans, Nikes, and snapback hats. Mingling with the spectators were performers dressed in banana-yellow jumpsuits and carrying dismembered crash test dummies. The performers encouraged audience members to reassemble the dummies and take selfies with them.

A$AP Rocky wore a crash test dummy mask while performing songs from his album *Testing*.

Suddenly an alarm blared as yellow lights flashed around the room. As people crowded around the cube, four men in yellow jumpsuits ripped away the cloth to reveal a massive Plexiglas tank. Inside the tank was exercise equipment, including a chin-up bar and weights. Along one wall stood a clear container filled with ice water. Something was submerged inside the ice water. People craned their necks to see what it was.

Over a loudspeaker, the male scientist said, "Successful completion of phase four, trial one."[1] This was the cue.

Sotheby's is known for its auctions of expensive items such as art.

A$AP Rocky emerged from the ice water. Dressed in a drenched Calvin Klein tuxedo, he had ice cubes in his braids and his teeth were chattering. This was the man the crowd had come to see—rapper, designer, fashion icon, and artist known for pushing boundaries. Rocky shook the ice from his hair and launched into his performance art piece, titled "Lab Rat."

> "I'm just a poetic young man, trying to express myself."[3]
> – A$AP Rocky

A DEMONSTRATION OF THE CREATIVE PROCESS

Audience members seemed both entertained and baffled as Rocky underwent a series of tests to illustrate his creative process. In robotic voices, the two scientists took turns ordering Rocky to complete tasks: remove wet clothes; dry off; put on a red Calvin Klein jumpsuit. Then the female scientist announced, "Phase four, trial two. The subject will use rhythm."

Rocky walked across the tank and pressed a foot pedal. The sound of a snare drum echoed through the room. The scientists asked if this rhythm made Rocky happy. "Not exactly," he replied. "Create new music," the scientists ordered.[2]

AN ICY TEST

During the "Lab Rat" performance, Rocky endured many tests. In one, the scientists commanded him to submerge his head in ice water. Bending over the side of the tank, Rocky immersed his head in the frigid water for 56 seconds. When he came up for air, the male scientist said, "The subject will do better," and ordered Rocky to go under again.[5]

Rocky did several chin-ups and looked around in confusion when the movement did not make music. Then Rocky yanked a pulley on the exercise machine, and a few seconds of electronic harmony filled the room. "Twenty percent dope," said the female scientist.[4]

Unsatisfied, Rocky continued to experiment. He pulled a lever, producing an organ sound. He yanked on the pulley again, layering the electronic harmony over the organ. He pushed a bar and a drumbeat began. Step by step, Rocky was creating new music.

The scientists permitted Rocky to collaborate. Three members of his hip-hop crew, the A$AP Mob, were escorted into the tank. With trial and error, they created a sound they liked, and soon all four men were rapping and dancing.

"Successful completion of phase two, trial two," the female scientist interrupted. The crew stopped dancing and left the tank. Rocky was alone again. Next, the scientists asked Rocky many questions, including whether he thought anyone would remember him in 100 years. When Rocky gave answers the scientists did not like, they barked out commands for him to follow such as moving his right arm or bowing his head. The questions and orders came faster and faster until the male scientist shouted, "Who are you?" Rocky screamed back, "I don't know!"[6]

RAP STARS AND PERFORMANCE ART

Performance art began in Europe in the early 1900s. Artists staged live exhibitions designed to prod audiences to think about radical ideas. Recently, performance art has worked its way into popular culture. In 2011, Lady Gaga arrived at the Grammy Awards in a giant egg. In 2013, Jay-Z rapped "Picasso Baby" while dancing around professional performance artist Marina Abramović at New York's Pace Gallery. A$AP Rocky's "Lab Rat" was another example of performance art. Critics question whether these musicians are trying to shake up society with radical ideas or trying to get attention.

As the show neared the 90-minute mark, dancers threw huge silver balloons into the tank. Rocky pressed his palms against the tank and stared at the audience as balloons pressed down around him. He pushed the balloons aside while looking for something.

Performers dressed as scientists hold up directions for the audience while Rocky performs music from *Testing*.

The dancers gyrated in a circle around the tank. While the audience's attention shifted to their performance, white smoke was pumped into the tank. Once the tank was full, the dancers slipped inside and were hidden by the smoke. Moments later, their faces and hands smashed up against the glass. They called for Rocky to open it.

The tank doors slid open and the dancers emerged. However, Rocky did not. Rainbow lights transformed the tank into a kaleidoscope of blue, green, red, and yellow. The lights illuminated only balloons. Then a spotlight fell on a wall next to the tank. The wall slid open to reveal a hidden stage. In the center was a turntable. Next to it stood Rocky, now dressed in a khaki jumpsuit. Smiling broadly, he held up his new album—*Testing*. The audience cheered.

WHO IS A$AP ROCKY?

A$AP Rocky emerged on the music scene in New York City in the summer of 2011 with the release of "Purple Swag." The music video drew lots of online attention because although Rocky was from New York, the song incorporated sounds and styles of Houston hip-hop. Two months later, Rocky released "Peso," a party

ROCKY ON FEARLESSNESS

In spring 2018, Sotheby's auction house in New York City interviewed modern artists who pushed boundaries with their work, including A$AP Rocky. When Rocky was asked what it meant to be fearless, he said breaking norms was dangerous for an artist. "You . . . kind of look crazy to people." Rocky ignored the danger and broke norms anyway because he had no desire to "preach the same story, the same song, I'd rather tell it my way."[7]

Rocky's success came after years of dedication to rapping and music production.

tune that was his breakthrough hit. The song was played regularly on radio stations and on MTV. By fall 2011, Rocky had a multimillion-dollar contract with a major record label.

In a few short years, the young artist breathed new life into New York hip-hop. Rocky's performance at Sotheby's proclaimed to the world that A$AP Rocky was not afraid to take risks. The fact that some people might not appreciate his performance art did not faze him. "It's not for everybody," Rocky said. "I can afford to be myself."[8] Over time, Rocky has gone from a street hustler to a rapper, actor, fashion icon, and entrepreneur. In his own words, he wants to do "Everything, everything."[9]

HARLEM ROOTS

On October 3, 1988, Rakim Mayers, later known by his rap name A$AP Rocky, was born in Harlem in New York City. Hip-hop influenced Rocky from the moment he was born. His parents, Duke Mayers and Renee Black, loved to listen to hip-hop music. Their favorite rapper was William Michael Griffith, better known as Rakim. This legendary artist of the 1990s was so skilled that his fans called him "The God."[1] Rocky's mother and father named their new son Rakim Mayers, calling him Rocky for short. Rocky claimed that when his parents named him after "The God," they jinxed him, "but in a good way."[2] Rocky has an older sister, Erika B., who was named for the other half of the hip-hop duo Eric B. & Rakim. He also had an older brother, Ricky, who taught Rocky to rap when he was only eight years old.

RAISED TO RAP

In the 1920s, Harlem had been the center of a wave of intellectual and artistic innovation known as the Harlem

Rocky has been immersed in hip-hop since a young age.

15

THE FIRST RAKIM

When Rocky was very young, his dad sat him in front of the television to watch Rakim's music videos so often that Rocky became confused. "I thought Rakim was my father," Rocky said.[3] Rakim rose to fame in the late 1980s as part of the rap duo Eric B. & Rakim. Their 1987 album *Paid in Full* was a turning point in the Golden Age of hip-hop. This era from the mid-1980s to the mid-1990s was known for musical quality, diversity, and innovation. But the best rappers, although lyrical, often had violent or aggressive lyrics. In contrast, Rakim delivered poetic, complex, and meaningful rhymes in a smooth and cool style, setting a new bar for emcees. After the duo broke up in 1992, Rakim went on to have a successful solo career in the late 1990s.

Renaissance. In the 1960s, the community was a hotbed for civil rights protests. For decades, Harlem was a self-sufficient community with a mostly African American population.

By the time Rocky was born, Harlem had seen an economic downturn. Jobs were scarce, and many people turned to selling drugs in order to survive. Gang violence also occurred frequently. Rocky's father supported the family by selling illegal drugs while Rocky's mother worked as a nursing assistant.

In the mid-1990s, Rocky's father moved the family to Pennsylvania. He continued to support the family by selling drugs. Then, when Rocky was 12 years old, Duke Mayers was sent to prison on a drug conviction.

Rocky says that when his father went to prison, their living situation quickly got worse.

Rocky's mother could not support the family, and they were evicted from their home. For the next couple years, Rocky and his mother and sister lived in homeless shelters in North Carolina and Alabama. Eventually, Rocky's mother decided to return to New York City. Rocky said, "We wanted to struggle in a place that we knew."[4]

TOUGH TIMES

Once back in New York, the family lived in a homeless shelter, which Rocky was embarrassed to admit to his friends. When friends

HARLEM RENAISSANCE

In the early 1900s, tens of thousands of African Americans left the South looking for better jobs and more equality. This movement, known as the Great Migration, led to 175,000 African Americans settling in Harlem, an area that was only three square miles (7.8 sq km). Between the end of World War I (1914–1918) and 1929, Harlem residents produced an explosion of cultural achievements. Artists used poetry, prose, sculpture, painting, jazz, opera, and dance to explore what it meant to be black in the United States. Writer Langston Hughes called the Harlem Renaissance "an expression of our individual dark-skinned selves."[5] The stock market crashed in 1929, signaling the onset of the Great Depression. During this decade-long period of economic decline, wages were low and unemployment was high. African American patrons no longer had the money to support artists, writers, and theatrical groups. Without funding, these creative people had to find other ways to make a living, and the Harlem Renaissance ended.

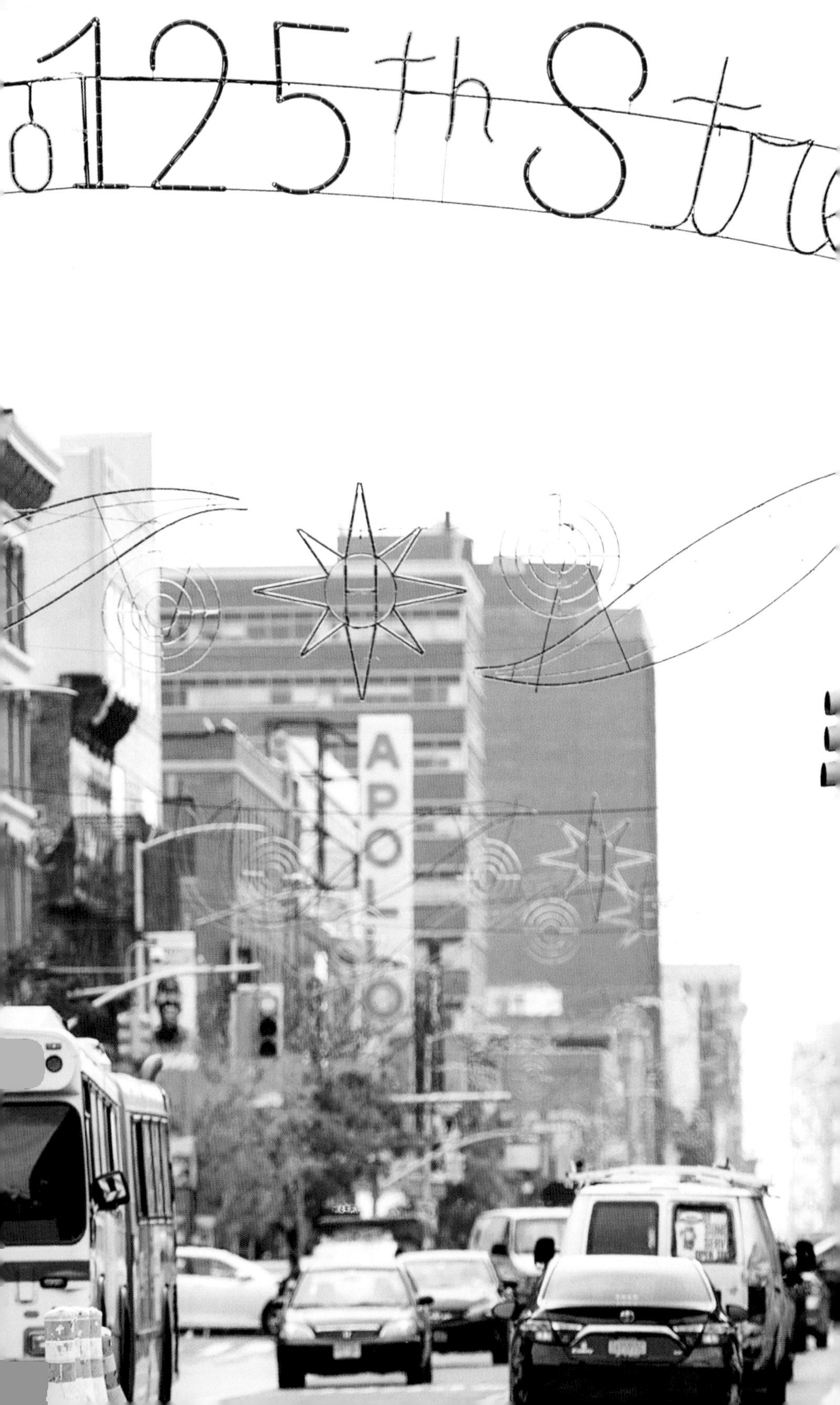
125th Stre
APOLLO

Harlem is in the northern part of Manhattan. The most famous street in Harlem is 125th Street.

asked if they could hang out at his house, he lied and said he could not have company.

Rocky had been back in New York for only a year when tragedy struck. His brother Ricky had followed their father into the drug trade, and on February 22, 2001, Ricky paid the ultimate price for this choice. He was shot and killed in a dispute with another drug dealer. Rocky was only 13 years old at the time, and the loss of his brother was devastating.

Despite the fact that the drug trade had almost destroyed his family, Rocky began selling marijuana and cocaine. He believed there were only two choices for young black men: hustle drugs or work at a fast food restaurant, and Rocky didn't want that kind of job.

However, selling drugs came with consequences. When he was 16, Rocky was arrested for drug possession and sent to the juvenile detention wing of Riker's Island

RAPPING BEHIND BARS

When Rocky was sent to Riker's Island Prison at 16 years old, he knew some of the other inmates because they were from Harlem. They encouraged Rocky to challenge other rappers in the prison in rap battles, and he won. Prison guards routinely gave inmates bread and jelly packets for free. When Rocky defeated the other rappers, he demanded jelly packets as his prize. The downside of victory was that when Rocky stored the jelly in his locker, ants got to it before he did.

"There was a lot of hard times [living in homeless shelters]. But it's not the end of the world because life is what you make it."[6]

— A$AP Rocky

Prison in New York. Rocky was luckier than many incarcerated teenagers. His grandmother cobbled together bail money and Rocky was released in two weeks. However, Rocky continued to support himself by selling drugs until his music career took off in 2011.

GOOD TIMES

Despite the tough times, Rocky has fond memories of growing up in Harlem. He attended Bayard Rustin High School for the Humanities, but came to school more to flirt with girls than to learn. Rocky and his friends often cut school to go window shopping at Barneys, a high-end department store. On weekends he went to cookouts and hung out on the street while listening to music.

As he grew up, Rocky was influenced by a wide range of hip-hop music. Hip-hop was born in New York City, but by the 2000s the genre had spread throughout the country. Over the years, each region developed its own style that made it stand out from the others. However, in the age of the internet, Rocky could access it all. He developed a unique rapping style that fused New York sounds with those from other parts of the country. Rocky later said he was influenced by "East Coast, West Coast, down South, Snoop Dogg, DMX,

NOT THE SAME HARLEM

Rocky only returns to Harlem once a year to visit his grandmother because the neighborhood depresses him. In the early 2000s, police cracked down on crime in Harlem. Developers later purchased vacant lots and abandoned buildings. Boutiques and chain stores replaced the old corner stores. But these improvements raised rents and drove out low income African Americans. This process is known as gentrification. A neighborhood that had been 98 percent black in the 1950s was only 60 percent black by 2015.[7] Rocky said the spirit of Harlem had changed. "It's just police on every corner," he said. "It's no culture."[8]

"The reason I connect with true artists is because we share compassion. Once you're compassionate about some s*** then all these stupid things are secondary, like money or success. Sometimes it's just about creating something."[9]
– A$AP Rocky

Rakim, for whom Rocky was named, was honored at the 2006 VH1 Hip-Hop Honors awards show.

Rakim. . . . It all sounded like rap to me."[10] Rocky might have just remained a recreational rapper. But in 2008, Rocky met A$AP Yams, a man who changed his life forever.

PRETTY FLACKO 2

Rocky often asks people to call him "Pretty Flacko 2." In a 2015 interview, he explained both the silly and serious origins of the name. *Flaco* is Spanish for skinny, and Rocky said, "I'm skinny and pretty, what can I say." But the real reason Rocky adopted the name is because Mos Def was the first rapper to use the nickname Pretty Flacko. Mos Def, an iconic New York rapper of the late 1990s, is Rocky's idol and mentor. Rocky adopted the name "Pretty Flacko" out of respect. When Rocky produces music, he often does it under the name "Lord Flacko" or "Lord Pretty Flacko Jodye II."[11]

THE A$AP MOB

Rocky's music might have remained a hobby if not for Steven Rodriguez, a young man with an influence among Harlem teens. Rodriguez was known as Yams. Rocky heard about Yams long before he met him. He said there was something mysterious about this guy who was popular and influential in the local hip-hop scene.

A$AP YAMS

Like Rocky, Yams grew up in Harlem. He was the son of a Puerto Rican father and a Dominican mother. Short and stocky with a large purple birthmark across one cheek, Yams became obsessed with hip-hop when he was still in elementary school. He spent all his free time listening to the radio or searching for music online.

Yams dropped out of high school and was hired as an intern at Diplomats Records. He developed a keen ear for musical talent and discovered self-recorded musicians and artists whose albums were produced by

Rocky's career took off after he met A$AP Yams and the rest of the A$AP Mob.

> "Yams is the hip-hop encyclopedia. He's no joke. That's one person I can't front on when it comes to music."[2]
>
> – A$AP Rocky

WHAT'S IN A NAME?

Yams chose the name A$AP. Yams did not want the group to be only focused on material possessions and money. He said, "We wanted to give it a real meaning and depth." Yams believed the name inspired the Mob members because it meant they were "destined for something . . . better."[3]

small, independent studios. Radio stations rarely played the music of unknown artists, but if Yams liked their sound, he spread the word. Yams became an astute observer of rappers, making note of what they did that was successful and what flopped. By age 16, Yams was the manager of a couple local music producers and sold their mixtapes to rappers looking for beats.

In 2006, Yams and two friends, Jabari Shelton and Illijah Ulanga, formed the rap group A$AP. The acronym stands for "Always Strive and Prosper."[1] Yams became A$AP Yams, Jabari became A$AP Bari, and Illijah called himself A$AP Illz. Together they became the A$AP Mob.

Yams spread the word that he was looking for more talent. The number of people in the Mob fluctuated over time. But the handful of core members shared a common vision. Their goal was to make A$AP Mob a giant in the world of hip-hop.

A$AP BARI

Yams and Jabari Shelton had been friends since childhood. As teenagers, they hung out with a group of guys who called themselves Team Nerd. In 2006, Yams and Bari decided the group wasn't their style any more, so they left Team Nerd and formed the A$AP Mob.

Bari introduced Rocky to Yams. Bari and Rocky had attended the same high school when Bari was a freshman and Rocky a senior, but they were not friends at that time. In 2007, the two men began to hang out. Rocky's rapping

A$AP BARI GUILTY OF SEXUAL ASSAULT

In January 2019, Jabari Shelton pled guilty to a charge of sexual assault. The charge stemmed from an incident at a hotel in London in 2017. During a party, Shelton made advances toward a woman who rejected him. That night, Shelton entered the woman's hotel room, yelled profanities at her, and struck her. After a video of the assault circulated on social media, Nike cancelled its contract with Shelton, who worked as a designer for the athletic wear company.

Early members of the A$AP Mob included, *clockwise from far left*, A$AP Ferg, A$AP Bari, A$AP Yams, A$AP Illz, A$AP Rocky, and A$AP Twelvyy.

skills impressed Bari, and he told Yams they should recruit him for the Mob. At the time, Yams was busy and kept putting Bari off. Finally, in 2008, Yams and Rocky met in person. After Rocky rapped for him, Yams realized Rocky had the looks, the flash, and the raps that could catapult A$AP Mob to a big stage.

A$AP ILLZ

Illijah Ulanga was only 15 years old when he became part of the original A$AP mob trio along with Yams and Bari. Unlike Rocky, who was a rapper before he became involved in fashion, Illz is a model first and foremost. His first modeling gigs were ad campaigns for the brands Stussy and Pyrex Vision. In 2014, one of Illz's dreams came true when he was hired to model the DKNY line in New York's Fashion Week.

Illz plays a behind-the-scenes role for A$AP Mob's music. In the words of a reporter for *Hypebeast*, Illz primarily serves as "both physical and spiritual support for the burgeoning careers of many of the Mob's members."[4]

A$AP FERG

Born and raised in Harlem, Darold Ferguson had known Rocky since they were young teens. Rocky hung out with a street crew called Million Dollar Babies and Ferg ran with a group called Harlem Envy. The two became friends and occasionally rapped together. After Rocky joined A$AP, he approached Ferg on the street one day and said they should make music together. Ferg joined the Mob and adopted the name A$AP Ferg.

In 2012, Ferg described his role in the group as "a brother, an innovator, [a] motivator." His goal was to put out a mixtape that would "have the world flipping upside down and doing somersaults."[5] Ferg helped Rocky do exactly that.

A$AP TY BEATS

Tyshaun Holloway moved to Harlem when he was eight. His father bought him music production equipment when Ty was 13. He used this technology to sample instrumental tracks and create new compositions. This is called making beats.

Ty and Rocky first connected on Facebook. Rocky was impressed with the younger boy's skills and invited him to join the Mob. He became known as A$AP Ty Beats.

Ty's goal was to create unique sounds. In 2011, he said, "I don't want to make beats like nobody else."[6] Ty's beats would help Rocky skyrocket from obscurity to fame.

ALWAYS SOMETHING TO LOOK FORWARD TO

More than a decade after its founding, A$AP Mob is going strong. The Mob is guided by the Black Book, a notebook in which Yams outlined plans for the group's future. Rocky said Yams's notes remind them that "He wanted everybody to move cohesively." A$AP Twelvyy described the Mob's cooperative nature in a 2017 interview. "Right now is meant for me to come in, then it's meant for Nast to come in, then it's meant for Addie to come in," he said. These friends have figured out how to take turns and share the spotlight. "We're always gonna have something to look forward to," Twelvyy said, "no matter what."[7]

A$AP TWELVYY

Jamel Phillips was born in Harlem but grew up in the Bronx. In 2005, he saw a social media post from Yams in which Yams said he was looking for the next great rapper out of Harlem. Phillips lived in the Bronx and did not rap, but he did not let this stop him. He messaged Yams, "I'm

the next best rapper out of Harlem."[8] The next day, Phillips went to Harlem and freestyled for Yams. Phillips was welcomed into the Mob and became A$AP Twelvyy.

Twelvyy said other talented young rappers did not want to join the Mob because Yams intended to promote one star at a time, and these guys did not want to wait their turn. Waiting did not bother Twelvyy. He was happy to help Rocky break into the big time.

A$AP NAST

Tairiq Devega is Rocky's cousin. When they were boys, they hung out, but when Rocky got older, the cousins drifted apart. After Bari and Rocky became friends, Rocky was often in his old hangouts, and Devega and Rocky reconnected. Rocky invited his cousin into the Mob, and Devega became A$AP Nast.

According to Nast, all Mob members pitched in to help Rocky produce his first album. There was no jealousy over Rocky getting the spotlight first. Nast said, "We're glad that he's kicking down the door for the rest of us to come in and shine."[9]

LOOKING FOR A NEW SOUND

Although the collective wasn't famous, the A$AP Mob was known on the streets of New York before Rocky belonged to the group. Each member worked on his own creative pursuits but also did collaborative projects. The group was committed to making the A$AP brand a dynasty of talent, not a one-man show. The A$AP Mob evolved at a time when New York hip-hop was stagnant. Little innovative music had emerged from the city in years. Because hip-hop was born in New York, the old styles of rap were considered sacred, but fans had grown bored. When Rocky joined the Mob, its members helped him create a sound that excited hip-hop fans.

A$AP MOB ALBUMS

In 2012, the Mob released its first mixtape, *Lord$ Never Worry*. In 2016, the group released its first full-length album, *Cozy Tapes Vol. 1: Friends*. It released the sequel, *Cozy Tapes Vol. 2: Too Cozy,* in 2017.

Other individual members also got their turn in the spotlight after A$AP Rocky. In 2013, A$AP Ferg's debut album, *Trap Lord,* was released. He was named Rookie of the Year at the Black Entertainment Television (BET) awards that year. A$AP Nast's breakthrough single "Trillamatic" was also released in 2013. In 2017, Twelvyy's first solo album, *12,* came out.

The syrupy rhythm of Rocky's first single "Purple Swag" was created by Ty Beats. A$AP Yams worked day after day to help Rocky cultivate his rap to incorporate lyrical styles from the South and Midwest. Sounding different from the New York rap that dominated hip-hop at the time would set Rocky apart. Mob members Clams Casino, A$AP Ty Beats, and SpaceGhostPurpp developed the hazy, slightly off-balanced sound of his debut mixtape *LIVE.LOVE.A$AP*. It was released in October 2011. When Rocky became famous nationally for his music, his success was the product of a team effort.

> **"Teamwork makes the dream work. . . . To share ideas and have support from those around you is crucial."[10]**
>
> *– A$AP Nast*

SOCIAL MEDIA SPREAD

For two years, Rocky and Yams worked on music almost every day. Yams urged Rocky to test different rhyme patterns and melodies to see which suited him best. What emerged was a New York rapper who sounded like he came from someplace else.

In 2010, Yams created a music blog on the social media site Tumblr. On this blog, he kept an archive of pictures, songs, and videos of hip-hop from different eras. Yams also uploaded music by emerging artists whose music did not fit neatly into a specific hip-hop subgenre. The site gained a lot of followers, and Yams became a musical tastemaker.

In early 2011, Rocky had a few songs ready for the public. Without telling listeners he had a professional connection with Rocky, Yams periodically played these songs on his blog. In this way, Rocky slowly built a

Rocky began performing for large crowds after the release of his first mixtape.

fan base. One such fan was Ty Holloway, now known as A$AP Ty Beats. After seeing the music video for Rocky's song "Get High" on YouTube, Ty messaged Rocky on Facebook. Ty explained that he was a beat maker, and Rocky agreed to listen to some of his work. The sample Ty sent Rocky changed the future of both men.

WU-TANG CLAN

People have compared the A$AP Mob to the Wu-Tang Clan, and Rocky is honored by the comparison. The Wu-Tang Clan was one of the most beloved rap groups of the early 1990s. The group's debut album, *Enter the Wu-Tang (36 Chambers)*, featured memorable hooks and beats that rappers still sample decades later. Rocky hopes A$AP Mob could become a classic too. In a 2012 interview with the *Guardian*, Rocky said, "Our plan is to stay productive, create a legacy and have longevity."[2]

PURPLE SWAG

When Rocky received Ty's composition, he turned up the volume, turned off the lights, closed his eyes, and let his raps flow. The song that emerged was "Purple Swag." The lyrics were about getting high on a purple cough syrup drink popularized by Houston rappers in the early 2000s. In the song, Rocky raps, "Purple swag / I'm in the zone / I'm getting throwed."[1]

A$AP Yams was profiled by the *New York Times* because of his contributions to the New York hip-hop scene.

The melody of "Purple Swag" drew on the sound of Houston's chopped-and-screwed music subgenre. Chopped-and-screwed rap is slowed down and remixed. This process changes a song's texture. Tones become richer. The music has a dreamlike quality, and the raps are paced at a slow tempo. Rocky believed hip-hop fans wanted a new sound that still felt traditional, and he was betting that "Purple Swag" was that sound.

The music video of "Purple Swag" shook the hip-hop scene. The video begins with a close-up of a white girl's face. She has blond hair and wears a gold grill on her lower teeth. As the song starts, the girl lip-syncs to a sample of rapper Mike Jones's 2004 single "Still Tippin'." The video then shifts to Rocky sitting on a couch with other members of the A$AP Mob. The scene resembles a 1990s rap video, as the Mob are smoking marijuana and drinking Colt 45 malt liquor.

The camera shifts between shots of Rocky and his friends and shots of the girl lip-syncing to Rocky's voice as he raps, "Everything is purple, everything is purple."[3] Yams put the music video on his blog in July 2011. Within 24 hours, the song had gone viral.

COUGH SYRUP

"Purple Swag" refers to the addictive cough syrup drink popularized by Houston rappers in the early 2000s, sometimes called Lean, Purple Drank, or Sizzurp. When someone drinks it, everything slows down and they experience a sense of calm. Musicians like DJ Screw, Pimp C, Macklemore, and Justin Bieber have referenced the drug in their songs, increasing its popularity. However, the cost of this creative crutch is high. Purple Drank is very addictive and, especially when mixed with alcohol or other drugs, often deadly.

CRITICS' REACTION

While fans loved "Purple Swag," some people inside the New York music industry did not. These critics did not like that Rocky was a New York rapper yet was releasing a song that sounded like it came from Houston. Mike Dean, Kanye West's record producer, tweeted, "we need some new [Houston] RAPPERS to blow up. WHY THE F*** THERE ALL THESE FAKE A** HOUSTON KNOCK OFF ARTISTS FROM UP NORTH AND WEST."[4]

Because hip-hop had been born in New York City, the old school way of thinking was that rap music from New York must stay pure. While people from other regions could take New York sounds and switch them up to fit their regional cultures, a New York rapper should never do the reverse. And none had—until A$AP Rocky came along. He was a Harlem rapper, but "Purple Swag" was a Houston sound that Rocky had reinterpreted for New York. This was a step too far for some people.

Yams defended their sound. In an interview with MTV, Yams said, "You gotta realize, we're a whole 'nother generation. We didn't just grow up on our sound

"PURPLE SWAG" CONTROVERSY

One reason the "Purple Swag" music video drew a lot of attention was because it featured a white girl lip-syncing the n-word. The girl's name is Anna, and she was Rocky's friend from Harlem. Some observers suggested that it wasn't controversial because she was only lip-syncing the lyrics. Rocky selected Anna specifically for the role. He described her as "a . . . chick from Harlem, and yes, she's Caucasian, gold grill shining."[5]

> "I would not consider myself to be a . . . real New York rapper. I don't even like New York rappers."[6]
>
> — A$AP Rocky, 2011

regionally. . . . If you look at all the greats, they all just a mixture of everything." He also replied to Dean's tweet, saying, "U def sound ignorant. The new generation is a melting pot of influences from everywhere."[7]

Rappers and hip-hop artists from around the United States have influenced Rocky's style and sound.

Rocky represented the new generation of rappers who had grown up in the age of the internet. He was not limited by geographical boundaries. Rocky could listen to hip-hop from all over the world. He did not need, nor did he want, to cling so tightly to the sounds and traditions of New York hip-hop.

THE DEAL

Approximately one month after he released "Purple Swag," Rocky released his next single, "Peso." The song quickly went from the internet to radio. "Peso" was a party song. Fans loved it, and record companies took notice. Several major companies got into a bidding war over Rocky. In October 2011, he signed a $3 million deal with Polo Grounds Music. Half of that money was for Rocky's solo work and the other half for the Mob's record label, A$AP Worldwide.

> "All my boys have money in their pockets, we're having fun, we all live like rock stars."[8]
> – A$AP Rocky

On October 31, 2011, Rocky released a mixtape titled *LIVE.LOVE.A$AP*. Critics were impressed. In an article for *Complex*, music critic Jacob Moore said, "The key to [Rocky's] appeal lies in his style and his ability to pick out a bunch of cool things, throw them in the melting pot, and cook up something that feels fresh." However, not all reviews were as positive. Another critic stated, "With the amount of hype currently surrounding the young Harlem emcee, he's pretty much destined to fail. There's really no place to go but down. . . . There's some good music on here, but I don't think it's the kind that justifies giving any artist $3 mill."[9]

Rocky was young and mostly unproven. While he received good press for *LIVE.LOVE.A$AP*, he needed to keep up the success on his debut full-length album. With the financing of Polo Grounds and the support of A$AP Mob, Rocky set to work on *LONG.LIVE.A$AP*.

"PESO" STYLE

"Peso" was released in August 2011. The song is about the lifestyle A$AP Mob lived in Harlem—trying to make money, look good, and get the girls. The lyrics flaunt Rocky's love of designer clothes, a style that later became central to his persona. In the song, Rocky references famous designers, rapping, "Raf Simons, Rick Owens usually what I'm dressed in."[10] "Peso" helped bring European high fashion into hip-hop culture.

44

"All I want is my credit, man. I just want to be an icon."[11]
— A$AP Rocky

TOUR AND DEBUT

The third annual Fashion's Night Out was held at the Versace Boutique on New York City's Fifth Avenue on September 8, 2011. At the event, members of the elite fashion world mingled with actors and models. Hip-hop superstar Drake played DJ, spinning records as everyone admired each other's cutting-edge clothing. Rocky was in the crowd, but few people knew who he was. Then, Drake called Rocky onto the stage and introduced him. According to Rocky, "[Drake] just showed me love. He was playing my records."[1]

While the release of Rocky's singles and mixtape drew the attention of fans and major record labels, Drake had even larger plans for Rocky. He gave Rocky the chance to appear on the national stage. Drake invited Rocky along on the four-month Club Paradise Tour in 2012.

TOURING WITH DRAKE

Drake's album *Take Care* was released in 2011, and he planned the Club Paradise Tour to support the album.

A$AP Rocky opened for Drake on the Club Paradise Tour.

Instead of asking famous rappers to join him, Drake invited two newcomers—Kendrick Lamar and A$AP Rocky. At this point, Rocky was only known by people who followed Yams's blog, so joining Drake was a major opportunity.

Rocky was surprised by Drake's invitation because the two men did not know each other personally. Drake explained that he was not interested in touring with people who were already famous just to sell more concert tickets. He wanted to give Rocky a chance. According to Rocky, he said, "I'm bring[ing] you out, do with it what you will. You take it to the moon from here."[2] Rocky was filled with gratitude toward Drake.

The exposure Rocky received from touring with Drake helped him rise quickly. Songs from his mixtape appeared

A$AP GRIZZLY

When Drake took Rocky on tour, he assumed Rocky could not afford a luxurious lifestyle. So when the group was going to a club for the evening, Drake delivered champagne and an envelope full of money to Rocky's hotel room. The generosity surprised Rocky, but Drake had his reasons for treating the young rapper well. He said it was rare to meet someone like Rocky, a person with both talent and a good mindset. Drake believed in fighting to promote music he believed in. Besides, he joked, "I'm just trying to earn the right to call myself A$AP Grizzly one day."[3]

Kendrick Lamar is a famous rapper who got his start alongside Drake and A$AP Rocky.

frequently on *Billboard*'s Hot 200 song chart. The Club Paradise Tour introduced Rocky to an audience of fans who might not have otherwise heard his music.

ScHoolboy Q is a West Coast rapper and a member of the hip-hop group Black Hippy along with Kendrick Lamar.

DEBUT ALBUM

Initially, Rocky announced his debut album would release on July 4, 2012. Expectations grew as the date drew nearer. Then Rocky pushed the release date back to September 11. As that date approached, Rocky announced another delay. The record would not come out until October 31. Then the date was changed to December. People wondered if A$AP Rocky was just another one-hit wonder.

To fend off these rumors, Rocky went on a promotional tour from September to November 2012 accompanied by rappers ScHoolboy Q and

TOUGH TIMES

Though Rocky had many successes in 2012, there were some setbacks as well. On July 19, 2012, Rocky was arguing with someone on a sidewalk in downtown Manhattan when two onlookers started taking photographs. Rocky fought them. The onlookers got some cuts and bruises and accused Rocky of trying to take their cameras during the assault. Rocky pled guilty to attempted larceny and had to pay a fine and perform community service. Then in December, Rocky's father passed away from pneumonia. His death occurred just a few weeks before the release of Rocky's debut album.

> Drake continued to collaborate with Rocky after the Club Paradise Tour.

Danny Brown. While on tour, he gave many interviews but remained mysterious about what fans should expect from the upcoming album. In an October radio interview, Rocky would only say he would not do anything expected. However, he added that his sound and production had improved since the release of the mixtape, so fans should expect better music on the album.

LONG.LIVE.A$AP was finally released on January 15, 2013. Songs on the album reflect the sounds of hip-hop centers across the country—New York; Houston; Los Angeles, California; Cleveland, Ohio; and Miami, Florida. The music also showcased styles from different hip-hop eras. When Rocky rapped over double- and triple-time beats on the song "PMW (All I Really Need)," he was displaying his skills at Trap, the hip-hop genre that first appeared in the early 2000s.

SINGING WITH RIHANNA

On September 6, 2012, Rocky performed the song "Cockiness (Remix)" with Rihanna at the MTV Video Music Awards at the Staples Center in Los Angeles. Rocky said he was not nervous until he saw Rihanna walking across the stage toward him. Rocky started to sweat, but then he reminded himself that he was meant to be on stage. When Rocky's verse began, the audience saw no signs of nervousness.

Rocky delivered his lines with a punch. The song "F*****' Problems" features Drake, 2 Chainz, and Kendrick Lamar. In the track, Rocky raps, "Never met a motherf***** fresh like me / All these motherf****** wanna dress like me."[4]

LONG.LIVE.A$AP was a hit with both music critics and fans. Jon Caramanica of the New York Times called Rocky "one of hip-hop's brightest new stars."[5] He praised Rocky for creating a new sound by interpreting music from across the country, rather than playing it safe by copying old hip-hop masters. Pitchfork described the album as "a triumph of craft and curation, preserving Rocky's immaculate taste while smartly upgrading his sound."[6]

SUDDENLY STARDOM

The track "Suddenly" on Rocky's debut album traced his roots from Harlem to stardom. The lyrics describe how he grew up with roaches on the wall and roaches on the dresser. This could be a reference to the insect, a slang term for the remains of a marijuana cigarette, or both. Rocky rapped about the fun stuff—cookouts and dirt bikes and dice games—and what he called everyday stuff—fistfights and gun deaths. He recalled how he had to borrow money from friends so he could eat, promising to pay them back when he became famous. Then, in the song, he raps, "Suddenly / Everything changed before my eyes."[7]

Rocky showed off his new sound during concerts around the United States.

One week after the album was released, *LONG.LIVE.A$AP* reached Number 1 on the *Billboard* 200 chart. On June 30, "F*****' Problems" won Best Collaboration award from BET, and it was also nominated for a Grammy Award. Rocky was well on his way to stardom, and fans eagerly awaited his next move.

AT LONG LAST

Rocky was busy working on his second album for most of 2014. To give fans a taste of what was coming, at midnight on October 3, 2014, Rocky released "Multiply," a single from the upcoming album. Fans liked it, and Rocky's career seemed poised to soar ever higher in 2015. Then, tragedy struck.

THE LOSS OF YAMS

On January 18, 2015, Rocky arrived at the Brooklyn apartment that Yams shared with A$AP Lou. Lou told Rocky something was wrong. Yams would not wake up. They went into Yams's bedroom, where he lay face down and was covered in vomit. When Rocky flipped Yams over and saw his friend's face, he knew they were too late to save him.

At a nearby hospital, doctors pronounced Yams dead. The A$AP Mob kept quiet about what killed their leader. Two months later, the New York medical examiner ruled Yams had died from an accidental overdose.

During the break between albums, Rocky branched out into other endeavors, including fashion and modeling.

57

On January 24, 2015, a week after Yams's death, Rocky was at the Sundance Film Festival in Park City, Utah. He was there to attend the premiere of the movie *Dope*.

Rocky had a small role in the film and was scheduled to kick off the after-party. On an outdoor stage, Rocky announced that his last song was dedicated to Yams. Rocky made it through the entire song but then had to leave the stage.

In a hotel room later that night, Rocky told a journalist that his heart had not been in the performance. He left the stage because he did not want to fake enthusiasm. "I just gotta keep it real. I can't front," he said.[1] That evening, Rocky flew back to New York to attend Yams's funeral.

Yams's death was a major blow to Rocky. The two men had shared a vision of the music they wanted to make. Yams was Rocky's sounding board, someone to

YAMS AND ADDICTION

Yams abused prescription drugs for years. At first he joked openly about it on Twitter, calling himself one of the Blackout Boyz. However, in 2011, Rocky confronted Yams about the damage the drugs were doing. After that, Yams concealed his use from his mother and his friends. Yams tried to get sober. A couple of times, he quit using for a month or two, and he went to rehab once. But ultimately Yams lost the battle to his addiction.

bounce ideas off. Yams also had connections in the music industry and a broad knowledge of hip-hop culture. He had managed business details so Rocky could concentrate on his music, and he helped Rocky shape his career strategies. Now, Rocky was in the middle of making a new album and the man he called his "truest, bestest friend" was gone.[2]

Members of the A$AP Mob performed a tribute concert to honor A$AP Yams after his death.

"MOVING AWAY FROM THE MAINSTREAM"

With the first album, Yams had convinced Rocky to make music that would be commercially successful. Rocky had to make a profit for Polo Grounds Music to justify the money he received. Rocky delivered. Tracks such as "Wild for the Night" and "F*****' Problems" were very popular. But by 2015, Rocky hated these songs and did not want to make more party music. He wanted to make music that was true to his heart and represented "something a little more honorable."[3]

It was hard to stay honorable when rich people were bombarding Rocky with offers to make music that he considered "just . . . terrible."[4] So after Yams's death, Rocky decided the only way to stay true to himself was to leave the United States and move to London, England.

London provided the isolation Rocky needed. He practically lived in a London music studio, even turning off his phone for several days at a time to avoid interruption. During this time, Rocky's creative spirit was recharged.

Still, rumors spread. Two years had passed since Rocky's previous album. Maybe Rocky had lost his touch. Maybe Yams had been the creative genius and without him, Rocky was lost. Rocky dismissed the gossip. "I'm an artist," he told one journalist. "When you're meant to hear about me, you're meant to hear about me. Only when I'm doing art."[5] Rocky was determined to produce music that mattered, regardless of how long it took.

As the recording on the new album wrapped up, Rocky emerged from seclusion. He had been invited to speak to the Oxford Union, the famous debating society of Oxford University. According to an article in the *Guardian*, Rocky was "moving away from the mainstream."[6] Rocky was embracing his namesake—Rakim. He said, "It's like the return of the God emcee, Rakim. I recognise that my name is Rakim. I'm taking ownership of it."[7]

Some people in that English audience challenged Rocky for not addressing important political issues in his music. In 2014, a white police officer shot and killed an unarmed African American

COLLABORATING WITH JOE FOX

Rocky was leaving his London music studio at 4:00 a.m. one morning when he was approached by Joe Fox, a musician who was experiencing homelessness. Fox had no idea Rocky was famous. He just wanted Rocky to purchase one of his CDs. Instead, Rocky asked Fox, who carried a guitar, to play a song for him right then. Rocky liked what he heard and wound up inviting Fox to move into his house and make music. Fox was featured on five songs on *AT.LONG.LAST.A$AP*.

Black Lives Matter is an activist group that advocates for racial equality and the end of police brutality against black people.

teenager named Michael Brown in Ferguson, Missouri. This event sparked days of protests. Activists from Black Lives Matter spoke out about how excessive force by police officers was endangering black communities. Some rappers addressed the issue in their music, but not Rocky. When a member of the debating society asked whether he had a duty to rap about political topics, Rocky said no: "Not everybody should . . . talk about political things just to stand out."[8]

That answer did not satisfy the audience. Another person asked Rocky if he had a responsibility to address racial violence. Again Rocky resisted. He said a white cop shooting a black man was "inevitable," and the more important issue was black on black crime.[9]

Rocky refuses to wear the label of socially conscious rapper. He even rapped about it in "Suddenly," saying, "Don't view me as no conscious cat, this ain't no conscious rap."[10] In a February 2019 interview, he said politics are a joke and he wanted nothing to do with them.

MONEY MOUTH

Rocky has diamonds implanted in his back teeth. He got the idea from a Romanian woman he dated for a time. She told Rocky about an elderly relative who had encountered tough times and was forced to leave her country. When the woman migrated to the United States, the only thing of value she had was her gold teeth. The woman pawned the gold and used the money to start her new life. So Rocky figured, "If the world ends at least my mouth will be valuable."[11]

AT.LONG.LAST.A$AP

The new album AT.LONG. LAST.A$AP was released on May 26, 2015. Rocky avoided the lively style of his previous hits such as "Goldie" and "Wild for the Night." The music features slower beats and a mix of whispers and echoes that leave the listener feeling light-headed.

Rocky's lyrics explored the theme of escape, including what drove him to London. In the track "M," Rocky raps, "Sometimes I wish I could get away and charter spaceships/To get away from my inhuman race with hearts of Satans."[12]

The album showcases a range of voices and sounds. Big-name musicians including Lil Wayne, Kanye West, Mos Def, and Rod Stewart appear on the record. The samples featured on AT.LONG.LAST.A$AP range from soul to Southern rock to indie rock.

A$AP Yams got the last word on the record. It ends with a recording of Yams in the studio talking about people trying to copy Rocky's music. "Y'all just gonna keep watching us at the beach and we just gonna keep surfing."[13]

Many reviewers liked what they heard. The Telegraph called the album "a woozy beauty."[14] Rolling Stone magazine said Rocky had "steely lyrics that often focus on inescapable truths."[15]

However, not everyone liked Rocky's new sound. Critics said his rapping was all over the place. Reviewer Kris Ex wrote in a review for Billboard that, "For all of the

Rita Ora is an English singer and songwriter who briefly dated A$AP Rocky.

sonic pleasures, much of *AT.LONG.LAST.A$AP*'s narrative is hard to swallow with a thinking mind—which makes it hip-hop at its finest, and its worst. . . . It's glaring when an album is so wide and deep and so narrow and shallow at the same time."[16]

Rocky's lyrics were characterized as random thoughts too often focused on drugs and sex. He had used illegal psychedelic drugs while recording, claiming they helped him create a vision for the work. One reviewer described *AT.LONG.LAST.A$AP* as a "psychedelic sprawl."[17]

Media outlets also criticized Rocky for using explicit and insulting lyrics about the singer Rita Ora in the song "Better Things." At first, Rocky tried to justify his actions. He had cheated on his girlfriend with Ora, and Ora had told people about it. "She had a big mouth," Rocky told a BBC reporter, implying that Ora deserved what she got.[18]

This explanation did not quiet Rocky's critics, so in July 2015, he offered a semi-apology. Rocky admitted, "The Rita thing was tasteless of me."[19]

This was not the first time Rocky had been called to task for lyrics that demeaned women. The same Oxford audience that challenged Rocky about race in 2015 had asked him whether rap music characterized women as sexual objects. "Maybe," Rocky said. "But we do it to men too." Then Rocky went on to distinguish two kinds of women. He said, "What I will say is, I'm 26, and I've met a lot of women, and I've met a lot of b******."[20] The implication was that one group should be treated with respect and the second group did not deserve it. Rocky seemed to be proving the point his critics were making—the rapper who claimed to love women did not always respect them.

Despite these criticisms, Rocky's fans liked *AT.LONG. LAST.A$AP*. The album went to Number 1 on the *Billboard* Top 200 chart. Rocky proved he could still make music, even without Yams. Now he was ready to explore other aspects of his creativity.

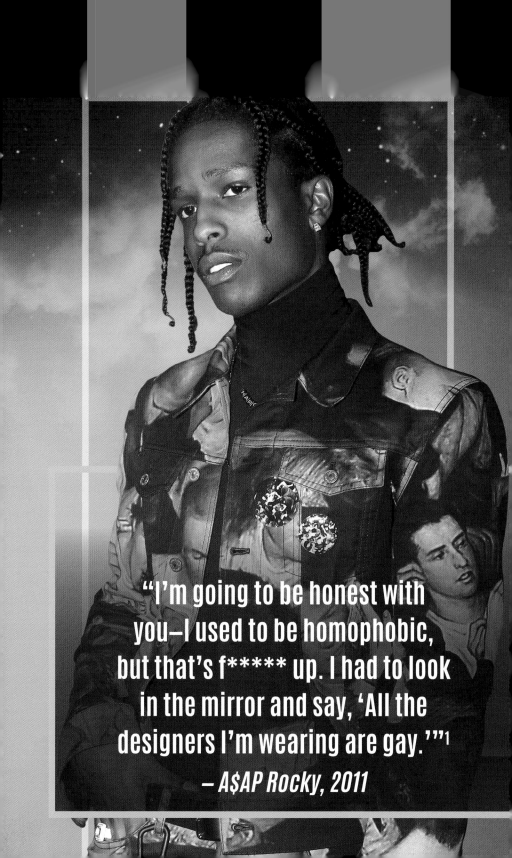

"I'm going to be honest with you—I used to be homophobic, but that's f***** up. I had to look in the mirror and say, 'All the designers I'm wearing are gay.'"[1]
– A$AP Rocky, 2011

FASHION ICON

The look of hip-hop artists has always mattered almost as much as their sound. Fashion expresses an artist's identity and is a mark of success. Hip-hop was the first music genre to associate with specific brands. When it came to hip-hop fashion in the 2010s, A$AP Rocky set the standard.

HARLEM INFLUENCE

Rocky's environment influenced his sense of style. He described New York City as a fashion center, and he believed Harlem implanted a "kind of mentality, a look, a pizzazz, a character" in anyone who grew up there.[2] Watching music videos as a kid in the 1990s made Rocky long to dress like the rappers on television. As a teen, Rocky was proud of his Guess, Old Navy, and Tommy Hilfiger apparel.

In his late teens, Rocky was able to afford higher quality clothes. It was at this time when his unique style was born—streetwear meets high-end fashion.

In 2017, Rocky attended a Christian Dior fashion show in Paris, France.

HIP-HOP FASHION EVOLUTION

When hip-hop music first began, luxury fashion designers had no desire to sell their clothing to rich rappers because of the stigma associated with their music. Designers refused to sell their clothing in Harlem and did not welcome rappers into their stores. Because of this, in the early 1990s, hip-hop artists started their own clothing lines. The Wu-Tang Clan launched Wu-Wear, and P. Diddy started the Sean John line. Baggy jeans, baseball jackets, and Timberland boots became hip-hop streetwear. Over the decades, rappers became mainstream celebrities, and their fans imitated their styles. Fashion designers began incorporating streetwear and hip-hop styles into their collections.

Rocky and his high school friends used to ride the subway downtown to shop in luxury boutiques. He would wear Air Jordans, a classic streetwear shoe, but pair it with a shirt by Raf Simons, a Belgian fashion designer. Or Rocky might sport a do-rag with skinny jeans. The do-rag was standard hip-hop headwear, but skinny jeans were not typical for the style.

In the early 2000s, men in Harlem wore wide-leg, baggy jeans. Other guys bullied Rocky because he dressed differently. However, Rocky defended himself with his fists. He also grew a tough skin, a strong identity, and a defined personal sense of style. "Some people look at me strange as hell," Rocky said. "That's cool. A lot of things I do . . . may not sit well at first, but eventually [people] aren't gonna have a choice but to get on the bandwagon."[3]

TRENDSETTER

The 2011 track "Peso" branded Rocky as a rapper with cutting edge style. In the song, Rocky rapped, "Swagger so impressive and I don't need a necklace," and "Our presence is a present, just to kick it is a blessing."[4] As Rocky gained fame, fans noted his natural comfort in high-fashion style, and they began to imitate him. Rocky became a trendsetter.

Rocky's eclectic wardrobe combined hip-hop and fashion in new ways in the 2010s.

"I felt like certain brands [understood streetwear], but they kind of gravitated toward skaters too much. Or certain brands got it, but they gravitated toward graffiti and art s*** too much."[5]

— A$AP Rocky, 2017

THE FACE OF DIOR HOMME

Rocky has long been a fan of Dior Homme, the menswear line of the luxury designer Christian Dior. On the track "Fashion Killa" from *LONG.LIVE.A$AP*, he rapped, "I adore your Dior."[6] On June 14, 2016, Rocky broke a major barrier when he became the first person of color to be the face of Dior's menswear line. Rocky showed that high-end fashions were not just for white people.

In the 1990s and early 2000s, young male rappers typically wore oversized, masculine workwear, such as Carhartt denim. By 2012, due in large part to Rocky's influence, rappers were more likely to wear a suit by European fashion designer Christian Dior. Rocky often combined both looks in the same outfit to send a message. Carhartt represented a humble, authentic rapper who knew his roots. Dior symbolized an artist successful enough to go anywhere.

Rocky did not become a fashion icon accidently. His team deliberately connected him to different audiences through music and fashion. In 2012, Rocky performed at the Black Scale boutique in Los Angeles, a

Dior is one of Rocky's favorite designers. He has worked with the designer label several times.

store that focused on dark streetwear with occult images. In 2013, he attended seven fashion shows in New York City during Fashion Week, rubbing elbows with well-dressed elites who had never listened to his music. In the music video for "Goldie," Rocky flashed a gold grill while wearing Christian Louboutin loafers. He was a master at fusing classic hip-hop styles with new looks.

COLLABORATIONS

After his second album was released in 2015, Rocky spent more time on fashion than music. He developed valuable relationships with important elite brands, and these

relationships cemented Rocky as a rapper with style. He
regularly attended the fashion shows of British designer
Jonathan Anderson. When Anderson opened his first
store in 2016, Rocky was one of his earliest customers.
After Rocky wore Anderson outfits in some of his music
videos, the designer invited Rocky to collaborate on a new
menswear collection.

Rocky adapted some of Anderson's designs into track
suits, knit hats, and fur "teddy" coats. He also created a

**Rocky wore clothes from his AWGE line when he
performed with singer Mary J. Blige at the 2017
BET Awards.**

logo for the clothes—JWA AWGE. These letters combine Anderson's initials (JWA) and the name of the agency Rocky spearheaded in 2014 (AWGE). AWGE is a secretive group for select people in music, fashion, television, film, and the lifestyle industries to collaborate on creative ideas and businesses. Anderson was pleased with Rocky's clothing designs. "I didn't try and control this process at all," Anderson said, "and I think the result is mega."[7]

Luxury fashions are not the only styles that appeal to Rocky. Under Armour is a sportswear brand typically associated with athletes. On September 15, 2017, the company announced a partnership with Rocky. Under Armour hoped the rapper would make their brand more attractive to nonathletes. In turn, Rocky was interested in the collaboration because the company's chief executive officer, Kevin Plank, shared his vision of improving inner

WHAT IS AWGE?

In 2014, Rocky and some friends formed a highly secretive group called AWGE. When asked to explain what the group was, Rocky said, "The first rule of AWGE is don't ask questions about AWGE."[8] When pressed, he would only say that AWGE was a collective of creative people including musicians, designers, and artists. The brand name AWGE appears on albums, music videos, and clothing. Rocky said the goal of AWGE was "Greatness, man."[9]

city communities. Rocky envisioned community centers where low-income families could be involved in art, fashion, music, and sports. The collaboration was intended to be a win-win relationship. Under Armour would get Rocky's clothing designs and branding, and Rocky would get Under Armour's money invested in poor urban neighborhoods.

FASHION OR MUSIC

In 2016 and 2017, Rocky spent so much time on fashion that some people questioned if he had the heart of a real musician. Rocky understood this reaction. However, he wanted fans to understand that he needed to take time away from music in order to develop his full career. "I'm a businessman. You gotta take me serious," he said.[10]

BABUSHKAS

Rocky showed up to the Los Angeles County Museum of Art's annual art and film gala in November 2018 wearing a floral silk scarf tied under his chin. The style resembled one worn by older women in the 1900s. Rocky paired the "babushka scarf" with huge shades and told reporters, "I look so handsome right now . . . I'm just encouraging all guys to wear babushkas from here on out."[11] Rocky later confessed that he started wearing the scarf because he had fallen from a scooter and gashed his cheek. Even when the cut healed, Rocky kept wearing the head scarf. He even included a song titled "Babushka" on his third album.

Rocky wanted people to know there was more to him than music. He identified as an artist in the broad sense of the word. An interviewer once asked Rocky what he would be if he could not be a rapper. Rocky's choice was an interior designer. "I love flowers. I think decor value . . . is important."[12]

FASHION ADVICE

In an interview, Rocky advised people to wear what suits them and not what is trendy. If a person looked and felt good in what they wore, their fashion would become a trend. Rocky recognized that everyone has a different body shape. He suggested that people worry less about style and "wear whatever makes you feel cozy."[14]

However, despite the time Rocky spent developing his fashion businesses, he was not done making music. "My whole life, I just wanted to be a rapper," he said in 2018.[13] The time had come for him to get back to making music.

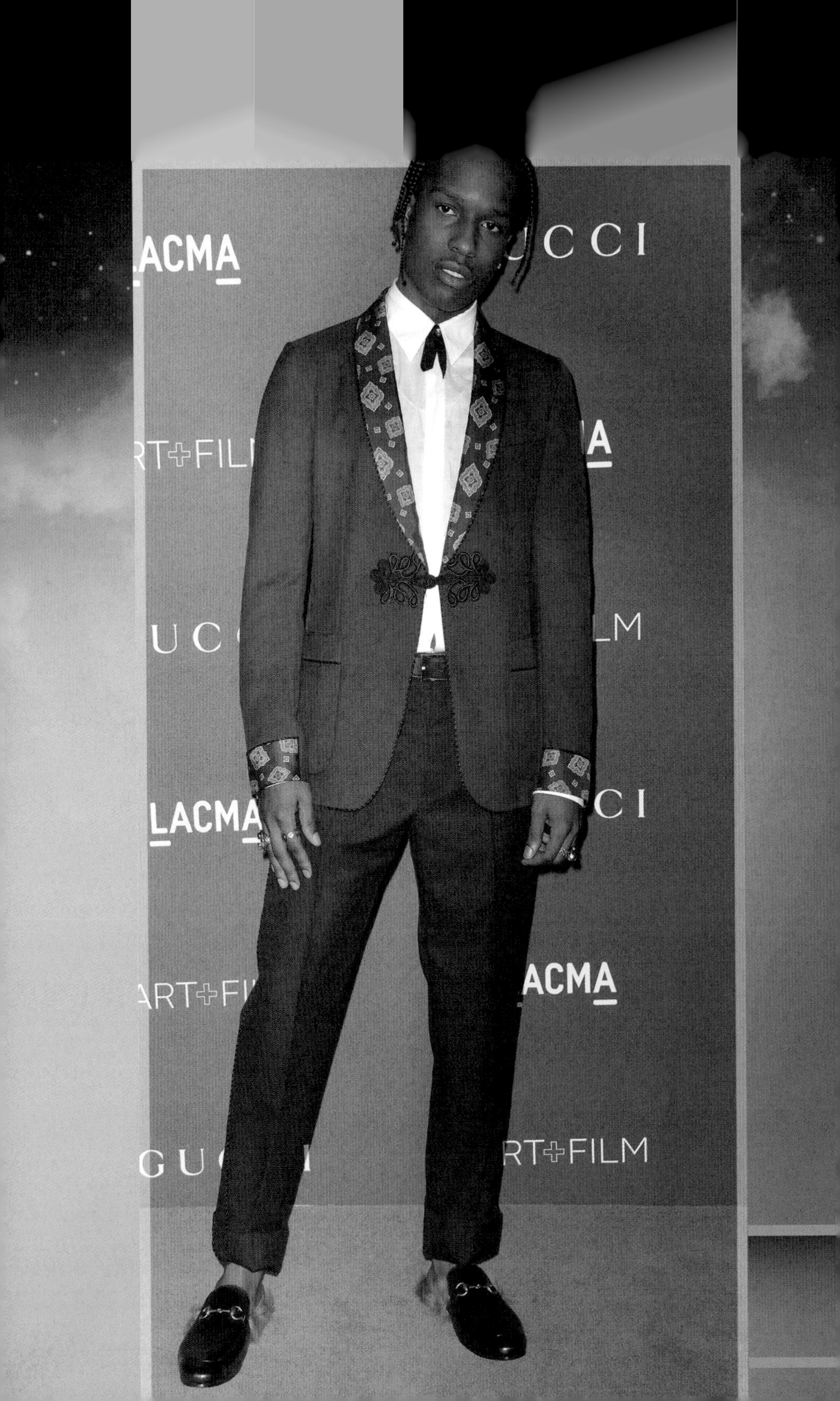
LACMA
UCCI
RT+FIL
A
UCC
LM
LACMA
CI
ART+FI
ACMA
GUC
RT+FILM

TESTING LIMITS

Fans waited three years for new music from A$AP Rocky after he released *AT.LONG.LAST.A$AP.* During this time, Rocky helped promote the careers of the A$AP Mob. A$AP Ant said Rocky wanted to "put his family in a better position."[1] Finally, in late January 2018, Rocky dropped three new songs online. Captions on each music video issued hints: "Testing coming soon" and "This is Just a Test."[2] Fans got the hint. A new album was on the horizon, and it was certain to be unusual.

AN EXPERIMENT

Rocky released his third album, *Testing*, on May 25, 2018. He chose this title because the process by which Rocky had made the album was one big experiment. He had always pushed the limits of his music, but on this album, Rocky intended to test things more deliberately.

Hallucinogenic drugs played a part in Rocky's creative process. He and British rapper Skepta took LSD prior to recording the single "Praise the Lord (Da Shine)."

After spending several years working on fashion projects, Rocky returned to music with his third album, *Testing*.

LSD

LSD is a hallucinogenic drug that causes the user to "trip," or experience mind-altering effects such as auditory and visual hallucinations. Many musicians, such as A$AP Rocky, Chance the Rapper, and the Beatles, have created music while under the influence of LSD. According to professor Philip Auslander from the Georgia Institute of Technology, this music "often feature[s] evocative . . . imagery . . . [as well as] surprising effects and juxtapositions of musical features you would not usually think go together."[4]

However, not everything about LSD is positive. Users can experience frightening or negative hallucinations. The drug can also cause anxiety and depression during and after use. In the United States, LSD is a Schedule I drug. This means it is illegal to use or distribute LSD. According to the US Drug Enforcement Administration (DEA), Schedule I drugs, such as LSD, heroin, and MDMA, have no use as medicine and are very likely to be abused.

Rocky believed the new sounds, sights, and sensations he discovered while recording were the result of being high on LSD. He wanted to incorporate drug-fueled discoveries into his new album. Rocky said, "Do you ever hear people when they describe that LSD experience and they tell you about colors that they never seen before? That's what I'm trying to describe. It's like the manifestation of drugs."[3]

Through lots of experimentation, Rocky created a hip-hop album with a collection of sounds. He sampled flute music for the first time on "Praise the Lord." The track "Calldrops" was an example of minimalist music. This style relies primarily on one instrument, often the guitar. In minimalism, chords are broken up and each note is played singly, and harmonic changes are slow. Rocky also used distorted vocals and warped samples to change his sound from previous albums.

Rocky's willingness to collaborate was also apparent in *Testing*. Rocky featured two new members of the Mob, Playboi Carti and Smooky MarGielaa. Other guest stars featured on the album included Frank Ocean, Kid Cudi, FKA twigs, Juicy J, and French Montana. Each artist had his or her own unique sound. For example, rapper Kid Cudi is known for humming in his own music, and he hummed on Rocky's album also. Rocky layered

FLUTE RAP

Flute sounds have been present in rap music since the genre began in the 1970s. However, in the last ten years, this woodwind instrument has been appearing much more frequently in top-selling tracks, both as synthesized samples and live performances. In addition to A$AP Rocky, other hip-hop artists including Future and Lizzo have incorporated flute into their sound. Future featured the flute on his 2017 track "Mask Off." Lizzo often plays the flute during her live performances, including her performance of "Truth Hurts" at the 2019 BET Awards. Additionally, one of Lizzo's first flute performances was an Instagram video where she covered "Mask Off."

the sounds of each artist between his own raps and the background beat.

REACTION TO TESTING

Rocky set the bar high when he hyped the new album, saying it would be the trend-setting album of 2018. After the album was released, critics agreed the album was experimental, but they disagreed on whether that was good or bad.

> "I feel like I'm one of the best contemporary artists out right now. My music is ahead of its time."[8]
> — A$AP Rocky, 2018

Some critics praised the innovative sounds Rocky created. A reviewer for *Highsnobiety* called *Testing* "an absolute triumph" and Rocky's "most thoughtful, most ambitious, and most rewarding project to date."[5] A writer for the website *Consequence of Sound* found the album "loud, frenetic, spastic, and about as vibrant as rap can be," and "a welcome addition to a genre that has become so occupied with . . . overly simplistic results."[6]

However, other critics believed Rocky's experiments on the album had failed. A writer from *Billboard* said Rocky was "style over substance."[7]

Testing did not do as well commercially as Rocky had hoped, either. The album debuted at Number 4 on *Billboard*'s Top 200 chart in the first week it was released. However, over the course of 2018, *Testing* came in at 125 on *Billboard*'s Top 200 albums of the year.

This lukewarm performance depressed Rocky. He told *Rolling Stone* magazine that he felt "emotionally discouraged. . . . I felt like the masses didn't get it at the start." But Rocky tried to remain optimistic. He was convinced that after people listened to the album a few times, they would conclude, "Oh my God, this is a masterpiece."[9] Armed with this attitude, Rocky went on tour.

INJURED GENERATION

The Injured Generation Tour began on January 8, 2019, in Minneapolis, Minnesota. It ended on February 6 in Kent, Washington, after a total of 18 concerts.

GROW UP AND GET A JOB

In 2017, Rocky starred in an advertising campaign for the German automobile manufacturer Mercedes Benz. The campaign was called "Grow Up." The ad began by listing the rules one must follow as they grow up. "Work hard." "Start a family." "Be a good parent." Rocky was featured in the ad about the rule "get a job."[10] The commercial traced Rocky's rise from a kid in the streets of Harlem to a rap star signing autographs as he leaned against his Mercedes.

Rocky said the tour's name was a metaphor. "It pertains to physically injured motherf****** and emotionally injured people, which is our generation."[11]

Rocky reprised his crash test dummy character from the Sotheby's performance during the Injured Generation tour.

When each concert began, Rocky entered the stage dressed as a crash test dummy. A computerized voice put Rocky through a series of ordeals, similar to his Sotheby's performance. The voice directed Rocky to take risks. While atop a car suspended above the stage, Rocky performed "Gunz N Butter." Inside a wrestling ring surrounded by fans, two semi-pro wrestlers grappled on a giant mat featuring a smiley face. Suddenly, Rocky materialized, dressed in AWGE track pants. With one punch, he knocked out the winning wrestler. Then, Rocky directed his fans to clear the area around the stage. This open space would serve as the mosh pit where people could jump and slam dance into each other with abandon. Once the mosh pit was full of writhing fans, Rocky climbed to the top rope of the ring and dove into the crowd.

The fans loved it. One fan said he would call the night a success if he did not go home with a black eye

> "You really can gain or possess or kind of borrow or take energy from other people. . . .You can't see the molecules, atoms, and protons, neutrons and all that s***, you can't see it right now. But it exists, right? . . . I swear to God, if it wasn't for that crowd and if it wasn't for them being lit, I would've sucked tonight."[12]
>
> – A$AP Rocky

During his set on the Injured Generation tour, Rocky climbed on a car that was suspended in the air. He rapped from his position on the car.

because the mosh pit was so full of excited and energetic people. In the live performance, the audience could feel Rocky's cockiness and charisma and the creative experience he had tried to bring to life on the *Testing* album.

Even critics of the album respected Rocky's performance on the Injured Generation Tour. A reviewer for *UPROXX* said, "Rocky's commitment to making himself a living crash dummy in the interest of entertainment is admirable."[13]

SAFETY FIRST

At a rave Rocky threw in Harlem, a fan under the influence of alcohol and drugs slipped on the subway platform when he was taking the train home. A train ran him over, and the young man lost both his legs. Rocky donated to an online fundraiser for the man and did a charity event where he auctioned off three classic cars, giving the proceeds to the injured man. Prior to going on his Injured Generation Tour, Rocky warned his fans to party more carefully, but he is not likely to take his own advice. At a sold-out concert in Chicago in January 2019, Rocky told a reporter, "I like to go crazy in a mosh, that's what I came here for!"[14]

ARTIST VS. CELEBRITY

A $AP Rocky believes there are two kinds of rappers—the celebrity and the artist. He wants to be considered a serious artist, but he is also very popular, and that makes him a celebrity. As an artist, Rocky wants to make a permanent mark on the music world. As a celebrity, he must please his fans and critics. Rocky's future depends in part on how he balances these two roles.

LEGACY

Rocky considers himself an artist ahead of his time. He believes his music carries a message, but he admits it is a message many people do not immediately understand. However, this fact does not faze Rocky because he is convinced his art has an important impact. In a 2018 interview, Rocky claimed he could recognize young

In 2018, Rocky and other celebrities attended the Art + Film Gala at the Los Angeles County Museum of Art.

rappers using the same sounds he was making back in 2011, and he thought this was amazing.

Rocky has already shown the world his influence as a fashion icon. Someday Rocky hopes to design furniture too. "I'm into mixing Victorian decor and pieces, like bronze and old trinkets, with new contemporary furniture from designers and artists," he told a reporter in 2018.[1] Rocky also aspires to be the creative director of a major fashion house. He wants young people to know that just because someone starts as a rapper, "you're not . . . limited to that name alone or just that title."[2]

THE FUTURE OF ROCKY AS A CELEBRITY

Despite fame and fortune, Rocky is determined to remain true to himself. He believes this is the key to his longevity in hip-hop. But what that means is likely to change over time.

Rocky made one major change in January 2019 when he announced he was going sober. It's no secret that Rocky has been a longtime drug user. In 2013, he proclaimed, "Weed is going to bring us together as a generation."[4] Turning 30 made Rocky take stock. He felt the amount of marijuana he was smoking was messing with his head. So for 2019, Rocky swore off alcohol, drugs, and sugar. The rapper insisted this was not a permanent lifestyle change. "I'm just taking a little break," he told a reporter. "I'll be right back to it."[5]

Rocky has defined his artistic style as being all about "the pursuit of happiness, spreading love," but not everyone agrees with this characterization.[6] In 2017, Rocky and A$AP Ferg released a video for the song "Wrong." In the video, Rocky wears a $700 Christian Dior T-shirt bearing the slogan, "We should all be feminists." Rocky and Dior both received backlash for this video because the song is about how Rocky and Ferg cheated on their girlfriends. Critics said Rocky was no feminist and had no right to wear such

> "You can be your own worst enemy. I say what I feel. That's going to come and bite me on the a** one day."[7]
> – A$AP Rocky

A$AP Ferg continued touring despite controversy on his music video with Rocky. In April 2019, he performed at the Something in the Water Music Festival in Virginia Beach, Virginia.

a shirt. They accused him of trying to make a profit off a popular slogan.

Rocky's vision of himself as someone who spreads love was also contradicted by his arrest for assault in Sweden on June 30, 2019. The rapper was in the middle of a European concert tour when he allegedly got into a fight with two men who were following the A$AP Mob.

A Swedish court ordered Rocky be held in detention for two weeks pending an investigation. A string of concerts from Moscow to Dublin had to be canceled. In August, the court found him guilty of assault and ordered him to pay a fine.

TOUGH STUNTMAN

In 2018, Rocky starred in *Monster*, the movie adaptation of a Walter Dean Meyers book about a teenager wrongfully imprisoned for robbery and murder. Rocky played a villain. Because the movie had a small budget, Rocky did his own stunts. In one fight scene, an actor wielding a gun clipped Rocky in the nose. When the director called for a break, Rocky dismissed his pounding head and the blood streaming down his face and said that they should continue filming. Later, it turned out that Rocky's nose was broken.

THE FUTURE OF ROCKY AS A RAPPER

The music Rocky makes will continue to evolve in sound

No matter what Rocky does in the future, he will continue to have avant-garde style.

and style because he plans to keep experimenting. Rocky considers himself in a unique category of rappers, one he described as occupying an "avant-garde art space." Proud that no other rappers make the kind of "eclectic" music he makes, Rocky intends to "perfect that sound more."[8]

Rocky's goal with his next album is to merge subgenres of rap. He wants to make music that bridges the sounds of "trip-hop, American grime rap, road rap, trap music . . . even French rap." No one knows what such a bridge will sound like, but Rocky is eager to investigate.

"I'm just testing sounds and waters. . . . It's the new wave. Let's get it."[9]

Whether critics like his musical experimentation does not concern Rocky. In a 2018 interview, he insisted he does not make music to get awards, but rather to move people. Rocky is most pleased when people tell him how his music, fashion, or words influenced their lives. "That's my Grammy, that's my Oscar, that's my everything."[10] In this respect, Rocky values the impact of his art and his legacy over the status of his celebrity.

Rocky has no desire to be the kind of rapper who reigns supreme over a subgenre or a geographical region. He does not want to be called the "King of New York" because kings have too much responsibility.[11] Rocky wants to be free to continue testing the limits of his own creativity.

ROCKY'S DIET

Rocky has not eaten meat since 2011. He does eat fish, so he is considered a pescatarian rather than a vegetarian. Rocky gave up meat in order to clean his "mind, body, and soul."[12] He was moved by the plight of animals slaughtered to feed humans. In an interview with the *Guardian*, he said, "Those chickens go through f****** torture before they're processed and s***, have all sorts of f****** steroids injected in them and everything."[13]

On May 17, 2019, rapper Juicy J tweeted that A$AP Rocky's "new album on the wayyyyyyyyyyy" and posted a photograph of Rocky and five fellow artists at 5:30 a.m. From their tired expressions, it looked like the men had pulled an all-nighter in the recording studio. In the tweet, Juicy J said Rocky had "cooked up a masterpiece."[14] However, fans and critics will determine if A$AP Rocky's latest experiment suits their taste.

> "I'm so blessed to be here. I could be dead right now. I could be in jail. I could be poor. I could be homeless still. But I'm here and I'm . . . happy as ever."[15]
>
> – A$AP Rocky

TIMELINE

1988

On October 3, Rakim Mayers, later known as A$AP Rocky, is born.

2008

Rocky meets A$AP Yams and joins the A$AP Mob.

2011

In July, A$AP Yams posts the music video for "Purple Swag" on his blog and it goes viral.

In August, "Peso" is available online and is quickly picked up by radio stations.

In October, Rocky signs a $3 million contract with Polo Grounds Music.

On October 31, Rocky releases his first mixtape, *LIVE.LOVE.A$AP.*

2012

Rocky performs an opening act for Drake's four-month Club Paradise Tour.

2013

On January 15, Rocky's debut album, *LONG.LIVE. A$AP* is released, and one week later, *LONG.LIVE.A$AP* is the Number 1 album on *Billboard*'s Top 200 list.

On June 30, Rocky wins the Best Collaboration award from BET for the song "F*****' Problems."

2015

On January 18, A$AP Yams dies from an accidental drug overdose.

On May 26, Rocky's second album, *AT.LONG.LAST.A$AP* is released.

2016

On June 14, Christian Dior announces that Rocky will be the cover model of its menswear line; he becomes the first person of color to represent the face of the luxury design company.

2017

On September 15, Rocky and Under Armour announce a partnership, in which Rocky designs and brands sportswear and Under Armour invests in community centers in inner city neighborhoods.

2018

On May 25, the album *Testing* is released.

2019

On January 8, Rocky begins the Injured Generation Tour.

FULL NAME
Rakim Mayers

DATE OF BIRTH
October 3, 1988

PLACE OF BIRTH
Harlem, New York City

PARENTS
Duke Mayers and Renee Black

EDUCATION
Graduated from Bayard Rustin High School for the Humanities

CAREER HIGHLIGHTS
A$AP Rocky released his first hit single, "Purple Swag," in 2011. Since then, he has released three full-length hip-hop albums. He also has collaborated on menswear fashion with designers Jonathan Anderson and Under Armour. Additionally, Rocky has acted in two movies: *Dope* (2015) and *Monster* (2018).

ALBUMS

LONG.LIVE.A$AP (2013), *AT.LONG.LAST.A$AP* (2015), and *Testing* (2018)

CONTRIBUTION TO HIP-HOP

When A$AP Rocky emerged on the New York City hip-hop scene in 2011, he breathed new life into a stale genre. Rather than adopting the traditional styles of New York rappers, Rocky fused sounds from other regions of the country and earlier eras of hip-hop into innovative new music. A$AP Rocky started a new trend in hip-hop culture by pairing typical streetwear with luxury fashion.

QUOTE

"I feel like I'm one of the best contemporary artists out right now. My music is ahead of its time."

—A$AP Rocky

BAIL

The temporary release of an imprisoned person on the condition that a certain amount of money has been deposited with the court to guarantee the accused person will show up for trial.

BLACK LIVES MATTER

A political and social activist group that was developed by African Americans in the United States in 2013; the group campaigns to reduce violence and racism against black people.

COLLECTIVE

A group of people working together.

COMMERCIALLY

Having to do with buying or selling and making a profit.

INTERN

A trainee who works, sometimes without pay, for a company in order to get experience.

LEGACY

The lasting influence of a person or thing.

MAINSTREAM

Ideas, attitudes, and activities that are considered normal.

MIXTAPE

A compilation of unreleased tracks, freestyle rap music, and DJ mixes of songs.

RENAISSANCE

A great revival of art, literature, and learning.

SAMPLE

A piece of recorded music used by DJs or producers to make new music.

SELECTED BIBLIOGRAPHY

Garvey, Meaghan. "A$AP Rocky: *At.Long.Last.A$AP*" *Pitchfork*, 29 May 2015, pitchfork.com. Accessed 9 Jul. 2019.

Hine, Samuel. "On Tour with A$AP Rocky, Who Wants You to Mosh Safely." *GQ*, 22 Jan. 2019, gq.com. Accessed 9 July 2019.

Pablo, J. "Meet the A$AP Mob: Talking to Ant, Ferg, J. Scott, Nast, Twelvyy, and Yams." *Village Voice*, 28 Aug. 2012, villagevoice.com. Accessed 9 Jul. 2019.

FURTHER READINGS

Burling, Alexis. *Drake: Hip-Hop Superstar*. Abdo, 2018.

Hawkins, Cordelia T. *Club Drugs*. Abdo, 2019.

ONLINE RESOURCES

 Booklinks
NONFICTION NETWORK
FREE! ONLINE NONFICTION RESOURCES

To learn more about A$AP Rocky, please visit abdobooklinks.com or scan this QR code. These links are routinely monitored and updated to provide the most current information available.

MORE INFORMATION

For more information on this subject, please contact or visit the following organizations:

BILLBOARD: CHARTS
billboard.com/charts

Billboard, a magazine about the music industry, posts weekly charts showcasing the top music around the world. The *Billboard* Hot 100 showcases the 100 songs of the week that had the most plays, downloads, and purchases.

SMITHSONIAN NATIONAL MUSEUM OF AFRICAN AMERICAN HISTORY AND CULTURE
1400 Constitution Avenue NW
Washington, DC 20560
nmaahc.si.edu

The Smithsonian National Museum of African American History and Culture has an exhibit titled Musical Crossroads. It traces the evolution of black music from the time Africans first arrived in America up to the present, including the evolution of hip-hop.

UNIVERSAL HIP-HOP MUSEUM
PO Box 6001
Bronx, New York 10451
uhhm.org

The Universal Hip-Hop Museum is scheduled to open in 2023 to coincide with the fiftieth anniversary of the birth of hip-hop. The goal of the museum is to preserve and celebrate both local and global hip-hop culture.

CHAPTER 1. BREAKING OUT OF THE BOX

1. "A$AP Rocky: Testing Presentation Full 'Lab Rat' Live Performance." *YouTube*, uploaded by *Pudding Music*, 20 May 2018, youtube.com. Accessed 9 Aug. 2019.

2. "A$AP Rocky: Testing Presentation."

3. "The 7 Best Outtakes from Our Interviews with A$AP Rocky and Ai Weiwei." *Sotheby's*, 10 May 2018, sothebys.com. Accessed 9 Aug. 2019.

4. "A$AP Rocky: Testing Presentation."

5. Jon Caramanica. "At Sotheby's, ASAP Rocky Breaks Out of the Box." *New York Times*, 25 May 2018, nytimes.com. Accessed 13 Aug. 2019.

6. "A$AP Rocky: Testing Presentation."

7. "Rapper and Producer A$AP Rocky and Artist Ai Weiwei on Art & Fearlessness." *Sotheby's*, sothebys.com. Accessed 9 Aug. 2019.

8. Caramanica, "ASAP Rocky Breaks Out of the Box."

9. Robert Marshall. "Hypetrak: A$AP Rocky – Always $trive and Prosper." *Hypebeast*, 10 Jan. 2012, hypebeast.com. Accessed 9 Aug. 2019.

CHAPTER 2. HARLEM ROOTS

1. Ime Ekpo. "Happy Birthday to the God MC: Rakim Allah." *Source*, 28 Jan. 2018, thesource.com. Accessed 9 Aug. 2019.

2. Jonah Weiner. "A$AP Rocky's Hard-Knock Life." *Rolling Stone*, 14 Mar. 2013, rollingstone.com. Accessed 9 Aug. 2019.

3. "ASAP Rocky Talks Drake, Growth, Rakim, Cam'Ron, Dipset." *YouTube*, uploaded by *Hard Knock TV*, 31 Oct. 2012, youtube.com. Accessed 9 Aug. 2019.

4. Eric Sundermann. "A$AP Rocky Lights Up the City," *Village Voice*, 23 Jan. 2013, villagevoice.com. Accessed 9 Aug. 2019.

5. "A New African American Identity: The Harlem Renaissance." *National Museum of African American History and Culture*, 7 July 2019, nmaahc.si.edu. Accessed 9 Aug. 2019.

6. Nadeska Alexis. "A$AP Rocky Takes Us to Hometown Harlem Block Where His Brother Was Shot." *MTV News*, 14 Nov. 2013, mtv.com. Accessed 9 Aug. 2019.

7. Tatiana Herrera. "The Changing Face of Harlem." *New York Amsterdam News*, 12 Jan. 2015, amsterdamnews.com. Accessed 9 Aug. 2019.

8. "ASAP Rocky (New York, 2015)." *Red Bull Music Academy*, 2015, redbullmusicacademy.com. Accessed 9 Aug. 2019.

9. Sanjiv Bhattacharya. "A$AP Rocky: Mr Dynamical." *Esquire*, 16 Oct. 2018, esquire.com. Accessed 9 Aug. 2019.

10. Weiner, "A$AP Rocky's Hard-Knock Life."

11. Caitlin Carter. "ASAP Rocky Talks New Album *A.L.L.A.* and More in Red Bull Music Academy Lecture." *Music Times*, 20 Apr. 2015, musisctimes.com. Accessed 9 Aug. 2019.

CHAPTER 3. THE A$AP MOB

1. Tshepo Mokoena. "A$AP Yams: The Business Brain behind A$AP Rocky's Fame." *Guardian*, 19 Jan. 2015, theguardian.com. Accessed 9 Aug. 2019.

2. Caitlin White. "ASAP Mob Founder ASAP Yams Dead at 26." *MTV News*, 18 Jan. 2015, mtv.com. Accessed 9 Aug. 2019.

3. Ernest Baker. "Who Is A$AP Mob?" *Complex*, 30 Jan. 2012, complex.com. Accessed 9 Aug. 2019.

4. Jake Woolf. "Essentials: A$AP Illz." *Hypebeast*, 16 Jan. 2013, hypebeast.com. Accessed 9 Aug. 2019.

5. Baker, "Who Is A$AP Mob?"

6. "A$AP Ty Beats Interview." *YouTube*, uploaded by *BlowHipHopTV*, 1 Dec. 2011, youtube.com. Accessed 9 Aug. 2019.

7. John Kennedy. "What's the Status of ASAP Mob?" *Complex*, 24 Aug. 2017, complex.com. Accessed 9 Aug. 2019.

8. "PT. 1 ASAP Mob's Twelvyy Tells Real ASAP History + Speaks about Meeting Yams." *YouTube*, uploaded by *Sway's Universe*, 4 Aug. 2017, youtube.com. Accessed 9 Aug. 2019.

9. J. Pablo. "Meet the A$AP Mob." *Village Voice*, 28 Aug. 2012, villagevoice.com. Accessed 9 Aug. 2019.

10. Tomas Fraser. "A$AP Nast on Fashion, Teamwork and Doing It for Yourself." *Dazed*, 26 May 2017, dazeddigital.com. Accessed 9 Aug. 2019.

CHAPTER 4. SOCIAL MEDIA SPREAD

1. "ASAP Rocky 'Purple Swag.'" *YouTube*, uploaded by *ASAPRockyUptown*, 5 July 2011, youtube.com. Accessed 12 Aug. 2019.

2. Paul MacInnes. "A$AP Rocky: We're Grungy but We Live Like Rock Stars." *Guardian*, 1 June 2012, theguardian.com. Accessed 12 Aug. 2019.

3. "ASAP Rocky 'Purple Swag.'"

4. @therealmikedean. "we need some new H TOWN RAPPERS to blow up." *Twitter*, 20 May 2012, 5:10 a.m., twitter.com. Accessed 12 Aug. 2019.

5. Robert Marshall. "Hypetrak: A$AP Rocky – Always $trive and Prosper." *Hypebeast*, 10 Jan. 2012, hypebeast.com. Accessed 12 Aug. 2019.

6. Jon Caramanica. "Thinking Globally, Rapping Locally." *New York Times*, 12 Oct. 2011, nytimes.com. Accessed 12 Aug. 2019.

7. Rob Markman. "A$AP Rocky Addresses Kanye West Producer's Criticism." *MTV News*, 23 May 2012, mtv.com. Accessed 12 Aug. 2019.

8. MacInnes, "A$AP Rocky: We're Grungy but We Live Like Rock Stars."

9. Insanul Ahmed. "What's the Consensus? The Internet's Top Tastemakers React to ASAP Rocky's 'Live.Love.ASAP.'" *Complex*, 4 Nov. 2011, complex.com. Accessed 12 Aug. 2019.

10. Will Welch. "A$AP Rocky Talks New Album, Under Armour Deal, and His Deep Love of Flowers." *GQ*, 23 Oct. 2017, gq.com. Accessed 12 Aug. 2019.

11. Eric Sundermann. "A$AP Rocky Lights Up the City," *Village Voice*, 23 Jan. 2013, villagevoice.com. Accessed 9 Aug. 2019.

CHAPTER 5. TOUR AND DEBUT

1. JustinM. "'Real Hip-Hop Is Back': An Interview with A$AP Rocky." *DJ Booth*, 21 Dec. 2011, djbooth.com. Accessed 12 Aug. 2019.

2. Phil Witmer. "Drake's Club Paradise Tour Predicted the Future of Rap Five Years Ago." *Vice*, 20 July 2017, vice.com. Accessed 12 Aug. 2019.

3. "Drake & ASAP Rocky Backstage of Club Paradise Tour @ Penn State." *YouTube,* uploaded by *BlowHipHopTV*, 12 Nov. 2011, youtube.com. Accessed 12 Aug. 2019.

4. "A$AP Rocky – F*****' Problems Lyrics." *Genius*, genius.com. Accessed 13 Aug. 2019.

5. Jon Caramanica. "Tweaking Rap's Rules, but with Respect." *New York Times*, 16 Jan. 2013, nytimes.com. Accessed 12 Aug. 2019.

6. Jayson Greene. "A$AP Rocky *LongLiveA$AP*." *Pitchfork*, 2 Jan. 2013, pitchfork.com. Accessed 12 Aug. 2019.

7. "A$AP Rocky – Suddenly Lyrics." *LyricsMode*, n.d., lyricsmode.com. Accessed 13 Aug. 2019.

CHAPTER 6. AT LONG LAST

1. Alex Gale. "Exclusive: A$AP Rocky Speaks In-Depth on Death of A$AP Yams for the First Time." *Billboard*, 25 Jan. 2015, billboard.com. Accessed 12 Aug. 2019.

2. Jon Caramanica. "ASAP Rocky, Dearly Missing ASAP Yams, Half of Their Formidable Hip-Hop Tag Team." *New York Times*, 22 Mar. 2015, nytimes.com. Accessed 12 Aug. 2019.

3. Nadeska Alexis. "A$AP Rocky Hates 'F*****' Problems' So Don't Expect That on *A.L.L.A.*" *MTV News*, 24 Mar. 2015, mtv.com. Accessed 12 Aug. 2019.

4. Harriet Smith Hughes. "A$AP Rocky at Oxford Union: 'I'm Scared of Women Now.'" *Guardian*, 18 June 2015, theguardian.com. Accessed 12 Aug. 2019.

5. Alexis, "A$AP Rocky Hates 'F*****' Problems.'"

6. Hughes, "A$AP Rocky at Oxford Union."

7. Hughes, "A$AP Rocky at Oxford Union."

8. Tom Goulding. "6 Things We Learned from A$AP Rocky's Talk at Oxford University." *Complex*, 17 June 2015, complex.com. Accessed 12 Aug. 2019.

9. Goulding, "6 Things We Learned."

10. "Suddenly Lyrics." *Lyrics.com*, n.d., lyrics.com. Accessed 13 Aug. 2019.

11. Ben Mitchell. "A$AP Rocky: What I've Learned." *Esquire*, 9 July 2015, esquire.com. Accessed 12 Aug. 2019.

12. Jon Caramanica. "Review: ASAP Rocky Returns to a Haze in 'At. Long.Last.ASAP.'" *New York Times*, 27 May 2015, nytimes.com. Accessed 12 Aug. 2019.

13. Caramanica, "Review: ASAP Rocky Returns to a Haze."

14. Neil McCormick. "A$AP Rocky, *At.Long.Last.ASAP*, Review: 'Big, Bold, Madly Ambitious.'" *Telegraph*, 27 May 2015, telegraph.co.uk. Accessed 12 Aug. 2019.

15. Jon Dolan. "*At.Long.Last.A$AP.*" *Rolling Stone*, 29 May 2015, rollingstone.com. Accessed 12 Aug. 2019.

16. Kris Ex. "A$AP Rocky's 'At.Long.Last.A$AP' Is the Perfect Experiment." *Billboard*, 29 May 2015, billboard.com. Accessed 12 Aug. 2019.

17. Dolan, "*At.Long.Last.A$AP.*"

18. Joe Lynch. "A$AP Rocky Explains Sexually Explicit Rita Ora Insult on New Album." *Billboard*, 27 May 2015, billboard.com. Accessed 12 Aug. 2019.

19. Lanre Bakare. "A$AP Rocky: 'Hanging Out with Rod Stewart Is Like Seeing Yourself 40 Years Older and White.'" *Guardian*, 2 July 2015. Accessed 12 Aug. 2019.

20. Hughes, "A$AP Rocky at Oxford Union."

CHAPTER 7. FASHION ICON

1. Henry Adaso. "A$AP Rocky Biography." *LiveAbout*, 24 May 2019, liveabout.com. Accessed 12 Aug. 2019.

2. "ASAP Rocky (New York, 2015)." *Red Bull Music Academy*, 2015, redbullmusicacademy.com. Accessed 12 Aug. 2019.

3. Jonah Weiner. "A$AP Rocky's Hard-Knock Life." *Rolling Stone*, 14 Mar. 2013, rollingstone.com. Accessed 9 Aug. 2019.

4. "A$AP Rocky – Peso Lyrics." *Genius*, genius.com. Accessed 13 Aug. 2019.

5. Bobby Hundreds. "'It's Not about Clothes': Bobby Hundreds Explains Why Streetwear Is a Culture, Not Just Product." *Complex*, 16 Feb. 2017, complex.com. Accessed 12 Aug. 2019.

6. Evan Minsker. "A$AP Rocky Is the New Face of Dior Homme." *Pitchfork*, 14 June 2016, pitchfork.com. Accessed 12 Aug. 2019.

7. Nick Remsen. "Up Close and Personal with Jonathan Anderson and A$AP Rocky's New Collab." *Vogue*, 6 June 2016, vogue.com. Accessed 12 Aug. 2019.

8. Matthew Schneier. "Jonathan Anderson Taps ASAP Rocky, Fan Turned Collaborator." *New York Times*, 8 June 2016, nytimes.com. Accessed 12 Aug. 2019.

9. Karizza Sanchez. "ASAP Rocky: All Together Now." *Complex*, May 2018, complex.com. Accessed 12 Aug. 2019.

10. Will Welch. "A$AP Rocky Talks New Album, Under Armour Deal, and His Deep Love of Flowers." *GQ*, 23 Oct. 2017, gq.com. Accessed 12 Aug. 2019.

11. Emma Hope Allwood. "We Stan A$AP Rocky's Gucci Russian Grandma Scarf." *Dazed*, 6 Nov. 2018, dazeddigital.com. Accessed 12 Aug. 2019.

12. Welch, "A$AP Rocky Talks."

13. Sanchez, "All Together Now."

14. Welch, "A$AP Rocky Talks."

CHAPTER 8. TESTING LIMITS

1. Karizza Sanchez. "ASAP Rocky: All Together Now." *Complex*, May 2018, complex.com. Accessed 13 Aug. 2019.

2. Sanchez, "All Together Now."

3. Sanchez, "All Together Now."

4. Suzannah Weiss. "This Is What LSD Does to a Musician's Creative Process." *Vice*, 13 Feb. 2018, vice.com. Accessed 13 Aug. 2019.

5. Jake Indiana. "'TESTING' Is the Album A$AP Rocky Was Born to Make." *Highsnobiety*, 29 May 2018, highsnobiety.com. Accessed 13 Aug. 2019.

6. Samuel Hine. "On Tour with A$AP Rocky, Who Wants You to Mosh Safely." *GQ*, 22 Jan. 2019, gq.com. Accessed 13 Aug. 2019.

7. Andreas Hale. "A$AP Rocky Returns with 'Testing,' His Most Experimental Album to Date." *Billboard*, 25 May 2018, billboard.com. Accessed 13 Aug. 2019.

8. Sanchez, "All Together Now."

9. Charles Holmes. "A$AP Rocky Felt 'Emotionally Discouraged' after Tepid Album Response." *Rolling Stone*, 24 Jan. 2019, rollingstone.com. Accessed 13 Aug. 2019.

10. Julien Rath. "Mercedes and A$AP Rocky Say It's Time for Young People to 'Grow Up' in a New Campaign." *Business Insider*, 8 Mar. 2017, businessinsider.com. Accessed 13 Aug. 2019.

11. Bansky Gonzalez. "A$AP Rocky Successfully Goes against the Grain on *Testing*." *Consequence of Sound*, 15 June 2018, consequenceofsound.net. Accessed 13 Aug. 2019.

12. Hine, "On Tour with A$AP Rocky."

13. Aaron Williams. "ASAP Rocky's Tour Stop at the Forum Found the Experimental Spirit That Was Missing on 'Testing.'" *UPROXX*, 6 Feb. 2019, uproxx.com. Accessed 13 Aug. 2019.

14. Hine, "On Tour with A$AP Rocky."

CHAPTER 9. ARTIST VS. CELEBRITY

1. Karizza Sanchez. "ASAP Rocky: All Together Now." *Complex*, May 2018, complex.com. Accessed 13 Aug. 2019.

2. Trace William Cowen. "Sounds Like the Next ASAP Rocky Album Will Be Even More Experimental." *Complex*, 7 June 2018, complex.com. Accessed 13 Aug. 2019.

3. Harriet Smith Hughes. "A$AP Rocky at Oxford Union: 'I'm Scared of Women Now.'" *Guardian*, 18 June 2015, theguardian.com. Accessed 13 Aug. 2019.

4. Jeff Weiss. "Q&A: A$AP Rocky on Sudden Fame, Relating to Kurt Cobain and Rihanna." *Rolling Stone*, 14 Jan. 2013, rollingstone.com. Accessed 13 Aug. 2019.

5. "A$AP Rocky Interview with the Cruz Show on Power 106." *A$AP Mob*, 5 Feb. 2019, asapmob.com. Accessed 13 Aug. 2019.

6. "A$AP Rocky on Tyler the Creator, New Relationship & the Injured Generation Tour." *YouTube*, uploaded by *Power 106 Los Angeles*, 31 Jan. 2019. Accessed 13 Aug. 2019.

7. Ben Mitchell. "A$AP Rocky: What I've Learned." *Esquire*, 9 July 2015, esquire.com. Accessed 12 Aug. 2019.

8. Cowen, "Sounds Like the Next ASAP Rocky Album Will Be Even More Experimental."

9. Cowen, "Sounds Like the Next ASAP Rocky Album Will Be Even More Experimental."

10. Sanchez, "All Together Now."

11. Reggie Ugwu. "15 Things You Probably Didn't Know about A$AP Rocky." *BuzzFeed News*, 8 May 2015, buzzfeed.com. Accessed 13 Aug. 2019.

12. Jonah Weiner. "A$AP Rocky: Harlem's Finest." *Rolling Stone*, 8 Dec. 2011. rollingstone.com. Accessed 13 Aug. 2019.

13. Adam Boult. "National Vegetarian Week: 20 Celebrities on Why They Gave Up Meat." *Telegraph*, 15 May 2017, telegraph.co.uk. Accessed 13 Aug. 2019.

14. Tara Mahadevan. "Juicy J Reveals New ASAP Rocky Album Is on the Way." *Complex*, 17 May 2019, complex.com. Accessed 13 Aug. 2019.

15. Sanchez, "All Together Now."

Judy Dodge Cummings is a writer from Wisconsin. She has written numerous books for children and teenagers. Her other titles about hip-hop include *Hip-Hop Culture* and *The Men of Hip-Hop*.